SCIENCE AND TECHNOLOGY
START-UP STARS

MILITARY Entrepreneurs

Heather C. Hudak

CRABTREE PUBLISHING COMPANY
WWW.CRABTREEBOOKS.COM

CRABTREE PUBLISHING COMPANY
WWW.CRABTREEBOOKS.COM

Author: Heather Hudak

Editors: Sarah Eason, Nancy Dickmann, Wendy Scavuzzo, and Petrice Custance

Proofreader and indexer: Wendy Scavuzzo

Editorial director: Kathy Middleton

Design: Clare Webber

Cover design and additional artwork: Clare Webber

Photo research: Rachel Blount

Production coordinator and Prepress technician: Tammy McGarr

Print coordinator: Katherine Berti

Consultant: David Hawksett

Produced for Crabtree Publishing Company by Calcium Creative

Photo Credits:

t=Top, tr=Top Right, tl=Top Left

Inside: Agility Robotics: pp. 16, 17; CyPhy: p. 15t; Dedrone: pp. 24t, 24b, 25t, 25b; Mobius Robotics LLC: Photo courtesy Mobius Bionics LLC. Used with permission: p. 6; RevMedx: pp. 4, 8bl; RevMedx/Brad Gilpin: pp. 8br, 9; Shutterstock: AlesiaKan: p. 26; Alexander Kirch: p. 28; PixOne: p. 29; Sozercem86: p. 21bl; Tonbo Imaging: pp. 20br, 21t; Torc 2017: pp. 12, 13t; U.S. Air Force: Kemberly Groue: pp. 3, 18; Susan A. Romano: p. 27; U.S. Army: pp. 11t, 22; Wikimedia Commons: Sgt. Scott M. Biscuiti: p. 19t; PHC (SW/NAC) Spike Call: p. 7b; Casey323: p. 10; Lance Cpl. Cesar Contreras: p. 14; Sgt. Sarah Dietz, U.S. Marine Corps: p. 13b; Honeywell: p. 19b; Petty Officer 3rd Class Jeffrey S. Viano, U.S. Navy: p. 15b; MilborneOne: p. 23; The Charles Machine Works: p. 11b; U.S. Air Force photo/Airman 1st Class Ashley Wood: p. 5b; Henri Manuel/Wellcome Images: p. 5t.

Cover: Shutterstock: Dmytro Zinkevych.

Library and Archives Canada Cataloguing in Publication

Hudak, Heather C., 1975-, author
　　Military entrepreneurs / Heather Hudak.

(Science and technology start-up stars)
Includes index.
Issued in print and electronic formats.
ISBN 978-0-7787-4422-1 (hardcover).--
ISBN 978-0-7787-4435-1 (softcover).--
ISBN 978-1-4271-2026-7 (HTML)

　　1. Military weapons--Technological innovations--Juvenile literature. 2. Military art and science--Technological innovations--Juvenile literature. 3. Defense industries--Technological innovations--Juvenile literature. 4. Entrepreneurship--Juvenile literature. I. Title.

UF500.H83 2018　　　　　　j623　　　　C2017-907705-8
　　　　　　　　　　　　　　　　　　　　C2017-907706-6

Library of Congress Cataloging-in-Publication Data

CIP available at the Library of Congress

Crabtree Publishing Company
www.crabtreebooks.com　　　　1-800-387-7650

Printed in the U.S.A./022018/CG20171220

Copyright © **2018 CRABTREE PUBLISHING COMPANY**. All rights reserved. No part of this publication may be reproduced, stored in a retrieval system or be transmitted in any form or by any means, electronic, mechanical, photocopying, recording, or otherwise, without the prior written permission of Crabtree Publishing Company. In Canada: We acknowledge the financial support of the Government of Canada through the Canada Book Fund for our publishing activities.

Published in Canada
Crabtree Publishing
616 Welland Ave.
St. Catharines, Ontario
L2M 5V6

Published in the United States
Crabtree Publishing
PMB 59051
350 Fifth Avenue, 59th Floor
New York, New York 10118

Published in the United Kingdom
Crabtree Publishing
Maritime House
Basin Road North, Hove
BN41 1WR

Published in Australia
Crabtree Publishing
3 Charles Street
Coburg North
VIC, 3058

CONTENTS

You Can Be an Entrepreneur! 4
Medical Miracles 6
Battlefield Start-Up Star: Andrew Barofsky 8
Radar Revolution 10
Self-Driving Start-Up Star: Michael Fleming 12
Robot Aware! 14
Robotics Start-Up Star: Jonathan Hurst 16
Candid Camera 18
Night Vision Start-Up Star: Arvind Lakshmikumar 20
Soldier-Robot Teams 22
Security Start-Up Star: Jörg Lamprecht 24
Entrepreneurs Changing the World 26
Your Start-Up Story 28
Glossary 30
Learning More 31
Index 32

YOU CAN BE AN ENTREPRENEUR!

Each day, military men and women risk their lives to help make the world a safer place. Many are wounded on the job. Their wounds could be fatal if they are not treated quickly. The **entrepreneurs** at RevMedx have an innovative way to help combat this problem. Their pocket-sized invention, called XSTAT®, consists of a syringe filled with tiny sponges that can help stop bleeding in just seconds.

Blood loss is the leading cause of death on the battlefield, so the military was quick to support RevMedx's project. One of the best things about XSTAT® is that it is made of affordable, readily available materials. "We haven't invented some exotic new material that's made out of platinum," explained the company's cofounder, Andrew Barofsky. Barofsky and his team are a great example of how entrepreneurs use science and technology to build a business that can change the world.

WHAT IS THE MILITARY?

The armed forces of a country make up its military. This may include the army, navy, coast guard, marines, and air force. The job of the military is to defend a country from potential threats. Threats can include anything from a natural disaster to war. The military works with businesses to provide weapons and aircraft, as well as services, such as medical support. Entrepreneurs, such as Andrew Barofsky, help the military develop new equipment and technology.

WHAT ARE ENTREPRENEURS AND START-UPS?

An entrepreneur is someone who plans, starts, and runs a business that provides **goods** or **services**. Entrepreneurs are people who take risks to develop new products and start new businesses. They sometimes have an original or **innovative** idea, then turn that idea into a business that supplies those goods or services. Start-ups are brand-new businesses created by entrepreneurs.

The sponges in an XSTAT® syringe can swell up to fill a wound in just 20 seconds.

INSPIRING STORIES

Early Thinkers

Many military entrepreneurs have invented products that are now used more widely. During World War I, the French and English military wanted to detect German **submarines** underwater. In 1917, the **physicist** Paul Langevin found a way to use sound waves to locate underwater objects. His invention paved the way for **ultrasound** technology. Ultrasound is commonly used by modern medical professionals to "see" inside the human body.

Paul Langevin was born in Paris, France, in 1872.

ENTREPRENEURS OF THE FUTURE

New technologies are changing our world at an incredible pace, and young people just like you could be the entrepreneurs of tomorrow. Who knows, perhaps you and your friends will follow in the footsteps of stars like Barofsky and Langevin, and create start-ups of your own!

People who work in the military do many different types of jobs, from soldiers and pilots to doctors, engineers, and cooks.

MEDICAL MIRACLES

On the battlefield, military medical professionals do not always have access to the supplies and equipment they would have in hospitals. This can make it difficult for them to treat the wounds of soldiers.

The military is always looking for new technologies to support its medical teams. Innovations in medical technology over the years have made a big difference in the way that the military is able to save the lives of its soldiers. These include storing blood for **transfusions**, blood–**clotting** bandages that help stop bleeding more effectively, and special **prosthetics**.

LUKE stands for "Life Under Kinetic Evolution." It also refers to the artificial hand worn by the *Star Wars* character Luke Skywalker.

PROSTHETICS

Thousands of soldiers have lost their limbs in battle. Many wear prosthetic limbs to help them perform everyday tasks, such as walking and eating. Inventor Dean Kamen found a way to make artificial limbs that are easier to use. His prosthetic arm, known as the LUKE arm, feels and moves almost like a real arm. It can move different parts at the same time, such as the fingers and wrist. It can pick up a wide range of items, from a coin to a drill. LUKE operates by responding to subtle muscle movements where the arm is attached.

Kamen's team first developed the technology as part of the Defense **Advanced Research Projects Agency (DARPA)** prosthetics program. In 2016, a start-up company called Mobius Bionics began manufacturing and selling the LUKE arm. DARPA is helping Mobius make the arm available to veterans and members of the military who have lost a limb.

TOURNIQUET TRANSFORMATION

Tourniquets are devices that stop blood flow by putting a lot of pressure on the wounded area. They have been used for centuries, but up until 2005, using them was a clumsy process that required the use of both hands. That all changed when the U.S. Army unveiled a new technology from a company called C.A.T. Resources. The small, lightweight Combat Application Tourniquet is easy to use and can be tied with just one hand if needed. The U.S. Army Institute of Research has rated it 100 percent effective. The tourniquet has reduced the number of deaths in the U.S. Army due to extreme blood loss by 85 percent.

INSPIRING STORIES

Battlefield Simulations

Members of the military can use medical training **simulations**, **mannequins**, holograms, and virtual reality to help train for real-life situations. Led by entrepreneur and **CEO** Oriel Herman, Israel-based start-up company Extreme Simulations works with the Israel Defense Forces (IDF) to help prepare soldiers for the battlefield. The team recreates the **chaos** of a war zone using **special effects** such as smoke and sirens. During a drill, wearable wounds, including a bleeding arm, send signals to special devices inside medical kits. This lets the trainees see whether the treatment they are applying is working.

Military simulations give soldiers a chance to train by experiencing lifelike combat zone situations.

7

BATTLEFIELD START-UP STAR:
ANDREW BAROFSKY

Every second counts with a gunshot wound. It can mean the difference between life and death for the victim. Traditionally, deep wounds are filled with **gauze** and bandages. This helps stop the blood flow. But it can take several minutes to do so. XSTAT® can do the same job in just 10 to 20 seconds. Andrew Barofsky, the president and CEO of RevMedx, claims that the product would be able to keep a victim alive long enough to get them to a hospital. Barofsky is an expert in scientific and medical research and development.

Many of the projects he has worked on have been funded by the U.S. Department of Defense. Over time, he began to develop a relationship with the United States military. When the military started to look for an alternative to gauze for treating gunshot wounds, staff turned to Barofsky's company RevMedx.

About 50 percent of battlefield deaths are caused by blood loss, but many could be prevented with innovations such as XSTAT®.

Andrew Barofsky has degrees in biochemistry, law, and business.

XSTAT® is ideal for treating soldiers who are not near a medical facility when they are wounded.

STRANGE INSPIRATION

At first, RevMedx wanted to create a foam solution similar to the kind that is used to fix a flat tire. Medics would spray on the foam, and it would expand to fill the wound. However, the large amount of blood pumping from the wound washed the foam away. Instead, the RevMedx team decided to use sponges. They compare their product to toy dinosaur eggs that expand into a dinosaur when they come into contact with water. Their product is effective because it stops the bleeding very quickly, even in **trauma** situations in which blood is leaving the body very quickly.

Each XSTAT® syringe contains 92 very absorbent sponges made from a plant-based material that will not break down when it comes into contact with blood. The sponges are **compressed** and covered with a special coating that helps clot blood and prevent infection. A single XSTAT® syringe can do the same job as five rolls of gauze. It can absorb up to 1 pint (0.57 l) of blood. XSTAT® syringes last for about four hours, giving medics plenty of time to get a patient to the hospital.

In April 2014, XSTAT® was approved for use on the battlefield. It was also one of *Popular Science*'s 2014 Invention Award winners. XSTAT®'s inventors hope that one day soon it will be used more widely to save lives.

RADAR REVOLUTION

Have you ever wondered how pilots land airplanes during a storm when they cannot see the runway? Or perhaps how ships move through dark waters without hitting coral and other underwater objects? The answer is radio detection and ranging, called **radar** for short. To locate nearby objects, airplanes and ships send a signal, or radar beam, made up of **radio waves**. If there are objects nearby, the beam will bounce off them and come back. The distance of the object from the airplane or ship determines how long it takes for the beam to bounce back.

Radar is extremely useful, and it can detect much more than just the distance of an object. Radar is also used to determine the speed, direction, and **altitude** of objects that are moving or standing still. These include vehicles, weather formations, **missiles**, and spaceships.

MILITARY HISTORY

In 1991, a Dutch company called Thales signed a contract with the Netherlands Defence Materiel Organisation (DMO). They agreed that Thales would design and build a long-range radar system called SMART-L. The system was first successfully tested in 1999. Over the years, Thales has produced many upgrades to the SMART-L system.

In 2017, Thales unveiled its latest version. The new radar **sensor** is called SMART-L MM/N, and it allows armed forces to detect threats from **ballistic missiles** well in advance. SMART-L MM/N can find a wide range of missile targets from as far as 1,243 miles (2,000 km) away. It can be used on ships or at bases on land.

Many ships, submarines, and aircraft were equipped with radar during World War II.

RADAR ON THE ROAD

Many companies are working on self-driving vehicles. Most of these rely on sensors, such as radar, to create a map of their surroundings. Radar is also used to track the speed of other nearby cars. This helps a vehicle know when to speed up and slow down to avoid collisions. The military is testing self-driving vehicles that could deliver supplies to soldiers or explore unsafe areas before sending in troops.

The Squad Mission Support System is a driverless vehicle that can carry heavy equipment for soldiers.

INSPIRING STORIES

Better Radar

Changing weather patterns and road conditions have made it difficult to build a driverless vehicle that works in all situations. Researchers at MIT Lincoln Library have developed a system called localizing ground-penetrating radar. It uses special radar sensors to detect a vehicle's exact location and create a map of the current road conditions. The United States military successfully tested the system over 1,000 miles (1,609 km) of challenging **terrain** in Afghanistan.

Ground-penetrating radar can detect rocks, cables, pipes, and other objects that are underground.

SELF-DRIVING START-UP STAR: MICHAEL FLEMING

Entrepreneur and Torc Robotics cofounder Michael Fleming is passionate about making the world a safer, better place. He has dedicated his life's work to designing and developing driverless vehicles for everyday life and for military situations. These vehicles can help prevent the tens of thousands of deaths and millions of injuries that result from motor vehicle accidents each year.

In the years since Michael Fleming founded Torc Robotics, it has grown from a small start-up to a company employing more than 80 people.

In 1997, Fleming began studying mechanical engineering at Virginia Tech. In 2005, he and a team of his fellow students took five top spots in a competition that tested driverless vehicles against one another. They won two awards in design and three awards in **autonomous** and navigation challenges.

That same year, the Virginia Tech team placed in the top 10 in the Department of Defense Advanced Research Projects Agency (DARPA) Grand Challenge. The competition was designed to promote the development of self-driving vehicles. DARPA was looking for fresh ideas to help trigger advances in technology. These successes drew a lot of attention to the work the students were doing.

STUDENT START-UP

Fleming wanted to make sure the work his team had done continued even after graduation. Fleming co-founded Torc Robotics two years after he graduated. His vision for the small start-up company included a continued partnership with Virginia Tech.

In 2007, Torc and Virginia Tech worked together to compete in the DARPA Urban Challenge. They built an autonomous Ford Escape that placed third in the competition. The partnership between Virginia Tech and Torc is still going strong today.

Torc has tested its self-driving cars by experimenting with specially modified Lexus vehicles.

UNMANNED MILITARY VEHICLES

In 2012, Torc Robotics began applying its cutting-edge technology to military and mining vehicles. Autonomous vehicles are especially useful for carrying out **missions** in dangerous situations without putting soldiers at risk. These situations include sweeping, or checking land, for mines. An operator simply programs a destination into Torc's Ground Unmanned Support Surrogate (GUSS), and the vehicle does the rest. It can even change routes by itself if it hits a dead end or receives a call for help from a remote operator.

GUSS works especially well when weather conditions are poor or roads are in rough shape. It is also very useful when there are many obstacles in the way. GUSS is ideal for taking supplies to soldiers and for moving wounded soldiers to safety. Fleming believes that many problems can be solved by using robotics and other advanced technology, such as GUSS.

The U.S. Marine Corps has tested the ability of the GUSS to perform in rough terrain.

ROBOT AWARE!

A robot is a machine that performs one or more tasks over and over again. It does this with great accuracy. Robots often perform tasks that are either difficult or dangerous for humans to do. In the military, these include looking for landmines, which are types of bombs in the ground. Some robots are remote-controlled. Others are autonomous, which means that they can act on their own.

Rather than putting human lives at risk, robots can be used to do many of the jobs soldiers do. They can fly planes, sail ships, and drive vehicles into battle. Over the past century, the military has been working with researchers to design and develop robots that can replace humans in risky situations.

ROBOT SOLDIERS

Nearly 90 nations are already using military robots in some way. Some of the most common U.S. military robots are the PackBot robots built by iRobot. The company was cofounded in 1990 by MIT graduates Colin Angle, Helen Greiner, and Rodney Brooks.

Soldiers use PackBots to find and defuse improvised explosive devices (IEDs).

The company is best known for the Roomba vacuum robot, but it started out building robots for space exploration and military tasks.

In 1998, iRobot began working with DARPA. The company released the iRobot PackBot in 2002. It is a lightweight robot that can be carried by hand and set up in less than two minutes. PackBots can perform all kinds of jobs, such as **surveillance**, detecting threats, and removing bombs. Since their early use in the Iraq and Afghanistan wars, thousands of iRobot PackBots have seen military action. Today, iRobot works on military robots, as well as robots that can help people do everyday tasks.

MODERN MILITARY ROBOTS

Unmanned aerial vehicles (UAVs), or **drones**, are the most common military robots in use today. One of the best-known UAVs is the RQ-1 Predator, which was first released in 1994. It has cameras for military observation. Today, companies are designing new types of UAVs. Currently, most small military drones have only enough battery power to last for minutes or hours. A company called CyPhy Works created the Persistent Aerial **Reconnaissance** and Communications (PARC) drone, which lasts for days or even weeks. In addition, it even runs in bad weather. Soldiers need very little training to learn how to use the PARC.

The PARC drone's reliability allows soldiers to focus on their mission rather than worry if their drone will work.

INSPIRING STORIES

Makers of MAST

There are robots that weigh less than a stick of butter! The Army Research Lab is working with various organizations to design and develop tiny autonomous robots that look more like insects or lizards. The project, known as Micro Autonomous Systems and Technology (MAST), launched in 2007. It aims to build micro-robots that can scope out dangerous situations before sending troops there.

The RQ-1 Predator was based on a design by Israeli Air Force engineer Abraham Karem.

ROBOTICS START-UP STAR:
JONATHAN HURST

As a child, Jonathan Hurst loved playing with Lego. But once he was done with a design, he tore it apart and started on a new one. By seventh grade, Hurst was using his design skills to build robots for a competition called the Science Olympiad.

Not much has changed since then. The materials and tools Hurst uses are more advanced, but he still loves to design and develop robots. He graduated from Carnegie Mellon University in Pittsburgh, Pennsylvania, with a **doctorate** degree in robotics. He took a job as an assistant professor at Oregon State University (OSU) in 2008. There, he developed a robotics laboratory and began working with students on science and technology projects.

INVENTING ATRIAS

At OSU, Hurst and a team of students designed a robot that could walk on two legs, instead of using wheels. They did this to demonstrate the ability of robots to copy human and animal activity. But the robot had many design **flaws**. More work was needed to perfect the design of a two-legged robot before it could be used in real situations.

In addition to his research with Agility Robotics, Jonathan Hurst continues to work as a professor at OSU.

OSU OFFSHOOT

Along with fellow Carnegie graduate Damion Shelton and OSU student Mikhail Jones, Hurst founded Agility Robotics in 2015. Agility spent 16 months inventing one of the most advanced two-legged robots in the world.

The robot, named Cassie, looks a lot like an ostrich. It can balance on its own, walk on any type of terrain, and be steered in different directions. It can run for six to eight hours on a single battery charge.

Cassie's design means that it can go places humans cannot. As a result, Cassie could be used in disaster areas, **nuclear** facilities, or other dangerous situations, such as areas with conflict. Agility Robotics' goal is for robots to go wherever people go. Having legs will allow these robots to do that. Hurst believes that this is just one of the ways that advancements in robotics will bring huge changes to our lives. He wants to change life for the better.

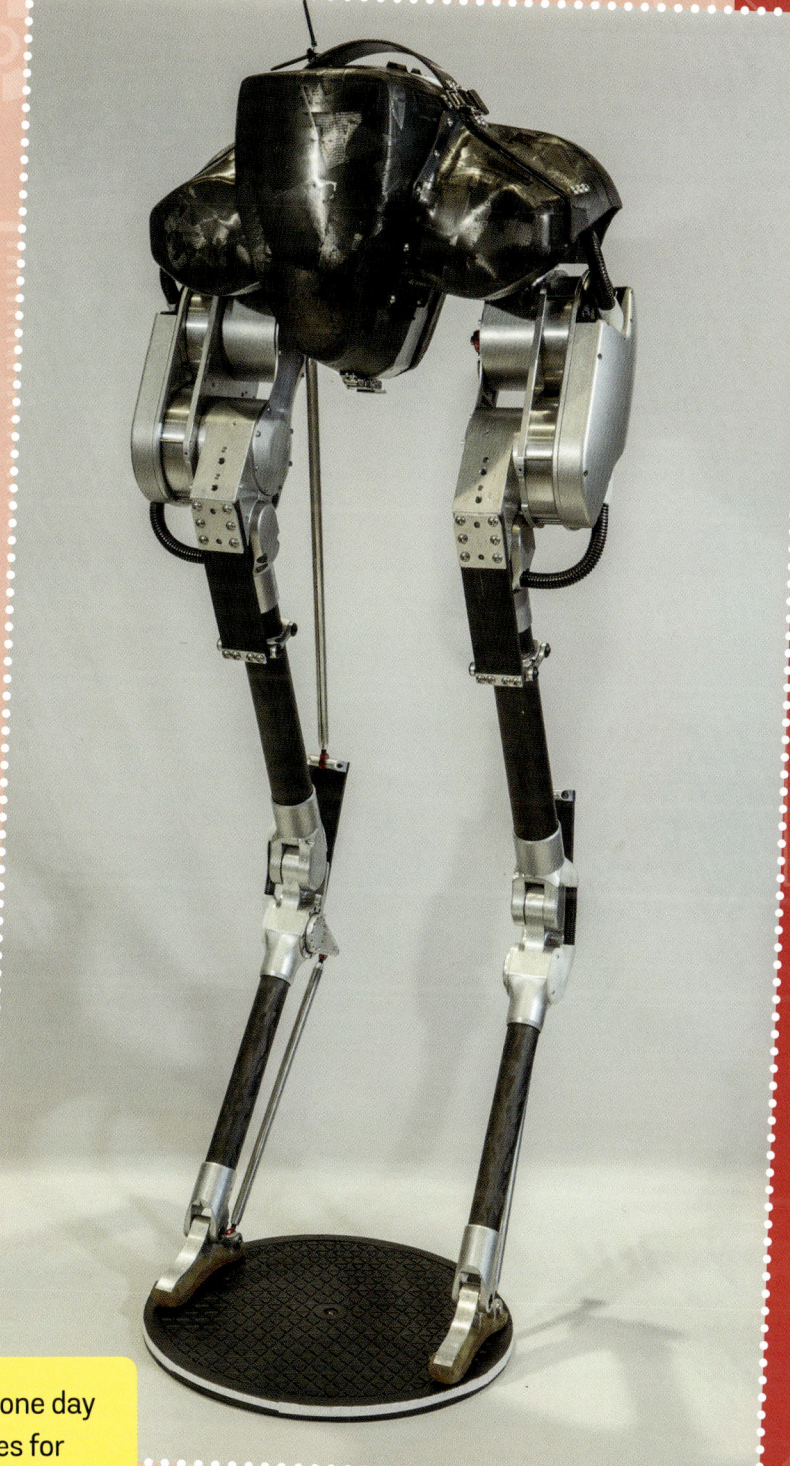

Agility Robotics hopes Cassie might one day be used to scope out unknown spaces for potential threats before sending in soldiers.

CANDID CAMERA

Have you ever tried to take a picture in a dark room? Without **artificial** light, it is hard to get a good shot. When you press the button on a camera, the **aperture** opens up to let light through the lens. If it is dark, and there is no light to let in, no picture will appear.

Thermographic cameras help solve this problem. They are able to detect heat from **infrared rays** that cannot be seen by the naked eye. All living beings and most machines give off heat. Thermographic cameras detect heat signals, then turn them into light images that people are able to see. This is called thermal imaging.

Thermographic cameras can notice small changes in temperature, allowing people to see in low-light and nighttime situations. This thermal imaging technology is used on planes, in security systems, and as part of military operations.

DIGITAL DISCOVERY

In the past, if soldiers wanted to spot a target at night, they had to use bright lights or flares. But that would also allow the target to see them. During the Korean War, researchers at the large American companies Honeywell and Texas Instruments applied their knowledge of infrared light to invent night vision technology. This used thermal imaging technology. It was a well-kept military secret for many years.

In 1958, a Swedish company called AGA released the first infrared camera for military use. It could be used to see through fog, rain, snow, and smoke. It helped soldiers see their opponents, even under the cover of night. Today, all types of military vehicles, from helicopters to battleships, are equipped with thermal imaging technology.

In a thermal image, the red, yellow, and orange areas are hot to warm, while the blue and purple areas are cool.

Israeli start-up AdaSky has a history of building innovative thermal imaging systems for the military. In 2017, the company announced it had developed thermal imaging cameras that can detect heat from people, animals, and objects on the road. AdaSky's solution can replace the cameras on self-driving cars that currently look for objects, since they do not work well in poor weather or low-light conditions.

Soldiers use thermal imaging to spot targets in low-light settings.

INSPIRING STORIES

Superhero Sight

Rain, snow, fog, and dust can block a helicopter pilot's view and make it hard to safely fly or land the aircraft. It is not uncommon for helicopters to hit the ground hard or even roll over. Through a partnership with DARPA, Honeywell has invented a technology called **synthetic** vision. It uses special sensors to create a 3-D image of an area. The image pops up on the pilot's screen so the helicopter can be safely landed.

Synthetic vision provides a computer-generated view of an area.

NIGHT VISION
START-UP STAR:
ARVIND LAKSHMIKUMAR

Arvind Lakshmikumar has been called the Tony Stark of new military technology, after the hero from the *Iron Man* comic books. Like Stark, Lakshmikumar is an entrepreneur with an eye for improving military operations. His start-up company, Tonbo Imaging, is based in Bengaluru, India. Tonbo Imaging provides the Indian military with high-end equipment.

Lakshmikumar graduated with Master's degrees in **software** systems and chemistry from Birla Institute of Technology and Science. He then moved to Ohio to get a degree in electrical engineering. From there, he made his way to Carnegie Mellon University in Pennsylvania, where he was a robotics researcher and a doctorate student. Finally, in 2008, Lakshmikumar decided to start his own company, and Tonbo Imaging was born.

DRAGONFLY EYES

Tonbo means "dragonfly" in Japanese. According to Lakshmikumar, his work on imaging has been inspired by dragonflies and their amazing eyesight. Each insect has 40,000 eyes that quickly process information. As a result, the dragonfly can move easily through low-light settings. Lakshmikumar wanted to find a way to give humans these same abilities. Using the dragonfly as an example, Tonbo began experimenting with different kinds of imaging systems.

Similar to a dragonfly's many eyes, Lakshmikumar wanted to find a way to give a camera multiple different lenses so that it could provide many images at once.

As a child, Arvind Lakshmikumar wanted to be a fighter pilot, but he changed his mind and pursued a career in science instead.

One of Tonbo's products is a handheld device that can help soldiers find targets at night or in bad weather.

OPTICAL IMPROVEMENT

Thanks to Tonbo's technology, soldiers can now see around corners and over obstacles without having to move into the sight of a possible enemy. Soldiers can hide behind a **blockade** and use a small thermal imaging device to locate the target. They no longer have to actually see the target or view real-time video feeds right on their weapons. "It is important for a soldier driving a tank to be able to see in bad weather conditions. The sensors are equally effective in day and night operations," Lakshmikumar said.

Tonbo works closely to support the military in India. However, other countries are lining up to get their hands on the start-up company's innovative devices. In the United States, DARPA, the U.S. Navy SEALs, and United States Special Operations Command are just a few of Tonbo's clients.

The head of a dragonfly is mostly made up of its eyes, so it can see nearly 360 degrees around.

SOLDIER-ROBOT TEAMS

Since World War II, any nation that took control of the skies had the best chances of winning a war. Now, there are new, more powerful technologies, such as long-range missiles and high-frequency radar. These technologies make it easy to locate enemy aircraft and attack with extreme accuracy.

Using robots and sensors gives soldiers the ability to see their targets from much farther away. Soldiers can also use manned-unmanned teaming, or MUM-T. This involves pairing manned aircraft and ground forces with unmanned autonomous systems, such as UAVs. Soldiers can use the information from the unmanned system to determine the fastest, safest way to engage with their targets. In the meantime, they can remain out of harm's way. MUM-T will play a very big role in future conflicts, since it puts robots in danger rather than soldiers.

U.S. ARMY EFFORTS

Modern MUM-T systems involve much more than remote-controlled robot bombs. Soldiers inside the manned aircraft, or on the ground, gather insider information about the enemy. They do this through live **footage** from cameras and sensors on unmanned vehicles. They can even take over the controls of the unmanned vehicles to fire their weapons or move them in a different direction.

DRONE PARTNERS

Since the 1980s, Schiebel has been making equipment for the U.S. Army to deal with battlefield mines. Based in Vienna, Austria, the company began experimenting with UAV technology in the 2000s. One of its most innovative designs, the CAMCOPTER® S-100,

The U.S. Army views MUM-T as a major part of its future missions.

has shown a great deal of promise for use in MUM-T. While most UAVs take off and land like traditional aircraft, the S-100 is more like a helicopter. It takes off and lands **vertically**. This means it does not need a long runway, so it is perfect for military missions when there is not enough space to land a plane. It can run during the day or at night, and on land or at sea.

In 2017, Schiebel partnered with Patria, a defence and aviation technology company. Patria's CANDL technology is being used to make a reliable link between the S-100 and manned military units. CANDL allows the MUM-T units to communicate over long distances, either air-to-ground or air-to-air.

The S-100 can be fitted with a lightweight missile.

INSPIRING STORIES

Battlefield Success

During the wars in Iraq and Afghanistan, Apache aircraft were teamed with unmanned aircraft for a variety of military operations. While the technology was still in its early stages, MUM-T proved successful on the battlefield. Researchers are looking to further improve the technology. In the future, soldiers may be able to use mobile devices to control the actions of a battlefield robot from anywhere. It could work in a similar way to playing a video game.

SECURITY START-UP STAR: JÖRG LAMPRECHT

Entrepreneur Jörg Lamprecht started his first company in 1996. At that time, he was studying math and computer sciences at the University of Kassel in Germany. Since then, he has started up three other successful companies, including one that builds drone defense systems.

Inspired by the need to protect our skies from spies and other threats, Lamprecht founded Dedrone. Based in San Francisco, California, the start-up company is the first in the world to offer an automated drone detection system. This would detect foreign, or unknown, drones in the sky high above us, which humans wouldn't usually be able to see.

Jörg Lamprecht raised $28 million in funding for Dedrone in less than two years.

Jörg Lamprecht is one of the most successful and experienced German entrepreneurs working today.

24

STAY OUT

It used to be enough for a company to put up a fence to keep out **trespassers**. But today, drones can fly over fences and into private areas. Lamprecht explains that drones can be used to hack into computers or devices to steal information, or even cause data systems to shut down.

To protect against this, Dedrone's DroneTracker system uses a system of cameras and sensors. These can detect approaching drones and send out alerts. Dedrone's airspace security system can take steps to defend against drones. When drones fly where they are not welcome, it can jam the drone's radio signals or **fog bomb** it.

MILITARY DRONES

The United States military has been developing drones for years. But the United States is not the only country in the world working on this technology. Russia, China, and other nations are designing drones for use in systems such as MUM-T.

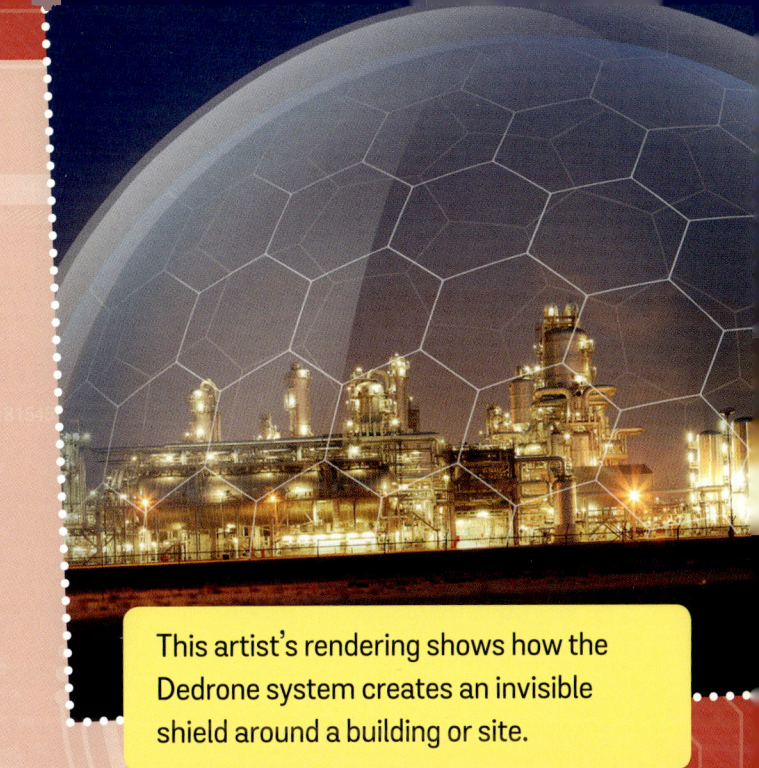

This artist's rendering shows how the Dedrone system creates an invisible shield around a building or site.

Drones can go places people and other equipment cannot. They can be used to spy on other governments or enemy forces. They can even be used to carry out military missions. Dedrone's system has already been able to detect rogue drones flying over U.S. military bases. Dedrone focuses on building military-grade security solutions to help the military protect itself against enemy drones.

Dedrone provided airspace security at the 2017 World Economic Forum in Davos, Switzerland.

Entrepreneurs Changing the World

Innovative ideas in science and technology, and the entrepreneurs who bring them to people around the world, have changed the way we live. As we continue to learn more about the world around us, our knowledge of science and technology also grows. It gives us the tools to design and develop even more exciting ideas.

The military of any nation is made up of armed forces. These forces protect and defend their countries against potential threats. Some threats involve opposing nations or **terrorist** groups. Others are the result of natural disasters, such as hurricanes or earthquakes. Armies, navies, and other military groups are constantly in need of more modern tools and equipment. They work with science and technology researchers, entrepreneurs, and organizations. Together, they design and develop innovative weapons, machines, and systems.

> Robotics is a great hobby for people with an interest in technology and engineering. Many young robotics designers take part in competitions to show their ideas.

Advances in military technology projects have a major impact on people around the world. Many military inventions are eventually made available for use in our daily lives. For example, ultrasound is now commonly used in hospitals around the world.

Entrepreneurs invest in ideas that they believe will help improve the world. Paul Langevin designed a solution to help the military succeed in World War II. Today, entrepreneurs such as Andrew Barofsky and Jonathan Hurst are creating technologies that will improve the way the military is able to win battles, save lives, and protect soldiers.

SCIENCE AND TECHNOLOGY ARE THE FUTURE

Think about the obstacles early military entrepreneurs may have faced while researching science and technology. They did not have the scientific knowledge or advanced technology that entrepreneurs use today. Still, they found ways to develop new science and technology ideas. What challenges will the military encounter in the future that entrepreneurs can help solve? Will there be more advanced systems for detecting enemy targets? Will cars and tanks be driving themselves into battle? Military science and technology entrepreneurs are always designing and developing new tools, systems, and equipment. Perhaps one day, you will be one of those entrepreneurs!

Each year, members of the Air Force tech team showcase experiments and hands-on activities at a Youth Day. It is hosted by the Organization of Black Aerospace Professionals. The event encourages youth to try out careers in science, technology, engineering, and math.

YOUR START-UP STORY

Military entrepreneurs are designing and developing innovative new products in many fields, from medicine to robotics. These help the military improve its ability to defend and protect people around the world.

TAKE THE START-UP CHALLENGE!

Being an entrepreneur takes of lot of hard work. It is not as simple as coming up with an idea. There are many factors entrepreneurs need to consider. You must figure out whether your idea helps solve a common problem people face. If it does, you need to find out how much people are willing to pay for your product or service. You also need to find out how much it would cost for you to make your product or provide your service.

Research the kinds of work other entrepreneurs are doing to see if it is the same as your idea. If there are similar solutions available already, how will your idea be different? Does it use more modern technology, or cost less to make?

Now it is your turn! Start your career as an entrepreneur by trying this activity!

Many types of drones are available for anyone to purchase in stores across the country.

START-UP CHALLENGE
CAN YOU HELP SECURE THE SKIES AGAINST DRONES?

Many start-up companies design UAVs. In the right settings, drones can be very helpful. However, in the wrong hands, they can also be a big concern. Some people worry that drones invade their privacy. Airlines have concerns about drones flying in the way of planes. Governments fear spies might use drones to get their hands on top-secret information.

Some entrepreneurs aim to secure the skies from unwanted drone activities. Could you think of a way to stop drones from invading people's privacy, interfering with planes, or even attacking the military? Here are some things to think about:

- What are some of the things drones can do that people cannot do?
- How does the military use drones?
- How are drones a threat to the military?
- What kind of devices or equipment could you use to help keep drones from entering private property?
- How can you use technology, such as radar and robots, to help?

Once you have come up with some ideas for securing the skies against drones, do some research to see if there are any other entrepreneurs with similar ideas. Why should a person choose your idea over the other ideas? Draw or use a computer to design your system and show it to your peers and classmates. Use their feedback to create a fool-proof drone protection system!

Some companies, such as Amazon, are thinking about using drones to quickly deliver packages. Do you think this is a good idea? Why or why not?

GLOSSARY

advanced New or ahead of its time in terms of progress and development

altitude The height of an object above ground level

aperture An opening or hole in a camera that light passes through

artificial Made by humans rather than occurring naturally

autonomous Having the ability to act on one's own

ballistic missiles Missiles that have a power source; they travel long distances in high, arched paths but eventually fall to the ground due to gravity

blockade Something that blocks people or vehicles from moving through a passageway

CEO (short for **Chief Executive Officer**) A person who is in charge of a company

chaos A state of total disorder and confusion

clotting Condensing and thickening to form a dense mass

compressed Flattened using pressure

doctorate The highest degree at a university

drones Unmanned vehicles, such as aircraft, that are controlled by remotes or onboard computers

entrepreneurs People who create a business and take on most of the risk to operate it

flaws Faults or imperfections

fog bomb Release fog to obscure a drone's sensors and confuse it

footage Unedited video recorded by a camera

gauze Thin, woven fabric that is often used to pack or dress wounds

goods Products; something made

infrared rays Parts of the electromagnetic spectrum that are invisible to the human eye but can be felt as heat

innovative Describing something that no one else has done before

mannequins Dummies or forms representing human bodies

missiles Objects that are launched at a target using force

missions Important assignments that often involve travel

nuclear Related to energy that is produced by splitting an atom

physicist A person who is an expert in the branch of science known as physics

prosthetics Artificial body parts, such as limbs or organs

radar A system that uses radio waves to detect the location of objects by sending out signals and "listening" as they bounce back

radio waves Parts of the electromagnetic spectrum that are used for communication across long distances

reconnaissance Checking out or observing an event or place to assess the situation before taking action

sensor A device that detects physical properties and responds to them

services Types of help or work that someone does for someone else

simulations Imitations or enactments of something

software A program that gets a computer to do things

special effects Illusions or tricks used to imitate real life

submarines Vehicles designed to operate underwater for long periods of time

surveillance Observing something closely or spying on the activities or movements of a person or group

synthetic Made by chemical processes rather than occurring naturally

terrain Land characterized by certain physical features

terrorist A person or group that uses violence to promote political or religious beliefs

thermographic Images produced using heat

tourniquets Devices used to stop blood flow by putting pressure on a wound

transfusions Transferring blood or fluids from one person to another

trauma Describes a traumatic injury, when medical attention is needed immediately

trespassers People who go to places without the owner's permission

ultrasound A method of using sounds that are too high for humans to hear to produce medical images

vertically Straight up and down or at a right angle to the ground, as opposed to forward and backward

LEARNING MORE

BOOKS

Bow, James. *Tech to Protect* (Techno Planet). Crabtree Publishing Company, 2018.

Burrows, Terry. *Robots, Drones, and Radar: Electronics Go to War*. Lerner Publishing Group, 2017.

Dougherty, Martin J. *Drones: An Illustrated Guide to the Unmanned Aircraft that Are Filling Our Skies*. Amber Books, 2015.

Larson, Kirsten W. *Military Robots* (Robotics in Our World). Amicus Ink, 2018.

Toren, Adam, and Matthew Toren. *Kidpreneurs: Young Entrepreneurs with Big Ideas!* Business Plus Media Group, 2016.

WEBSITES

Defense Advanced Research Projects Agency (DARPA)

www.darpa.mil/our-research

Find out about the exciting projects DARPA is working on.

Drone Lab

mydronelab.com/blog/what-is-a-drone.html

Find out all about what drones are and how they work.

HowStuffWorks

https://science.howstuffworks.com/radar.htm

Learn all about how radar works.

TeachingKidsBusiness.com

www.teachingkidsbusiness.com

Learn everything you need to know about becoming an entrepreneur.

INDEX

AdaSky 19
AGA 18
Agility Robotics 16–17
Air Force 27
airspace security 24–25, 28–29
artificial limbs 6–7

Barofsky, Andrew 4, 8–9
blood loss 4, 8–9
blood transfusions 6

CAMCOPTER® S-100 22–23
CANDL technology 23
Cassie 17
C.A.T. Resources 7
Combat Application Tourniquet 7
CyPhy Works 15

DARPA 7, 12, 14, 19
Dedrone 24–25
dragonfly eyes 20, 21
driverless vehicles 11, 12–13, 19
drone detection 24–25, 28–29
drone security challenge 28–29
drones 15, 24–25, 28–29
DroneTracker 25

entrepreneurs defined 4
explosives 14, 22
Extreme Simulations 7

Fleming, Michael 12–13
fund-raising 24

Ground Unmanned Support Surrogate (GUSS) 13

Herman, Oriel 7
Hurst, Jonathan 16–17

iRobot 14

Kamen, Dean 6
Karem, Abraham 15

Lakshmikumar, Arvind 20–21
Lamprecht, Jörg 24–25
Langevin, Paul 5, 27
localizing ground-penetrating radar 11
LUKE arm 6, 7

MAST 15
medical innovations 4, 6–7, 8–9
military simulations 7
Mobius Bionics 7
motor vehicle accidents 12
MUM-T 22–23, 25

night vision 20–21, 24–25

PackBots 14
PARC drones 15
Patria 23
prosthetics 6–7

radar 10–11
RevMedx 4, 8–9
robotics 14–15, 22–23, 26
rogue drones 25
RQ-1 Predator 15

Schiebel 22–23
SMART-L radar systems 10
Squad Mission Support System 11
start-ups defined 4
synthetic vision 19
syringes 4, 9

Thales 10
thermal imaging 18–19, 21
thermographic cameras 18
threats 4, 10, 14, 17, 24, 26
Tonbo Imaging 20–21
Torc Robotics 12–13
tourniquets 7

ultrasound 5, 27
unmanned aerial vehicles (UAVs) 15, 22–23

World War I 5
World War II 10, 22, 27
wounds 4, 6, 8–9

XSTAT® 4, 8, 9

Youth Day 27

ABOUT THE AUTHOR

Heather C. Hudak has written hundreds of books for children and edited thousands more. She loves learning about new topics, traveling the world, and spending time with her husband and many pets.